The Little Corporal: A Comic Opera, In Three Acts

Harry Bache Smith

In the interest of creating a more extensive selection of rare historical book reprints, we have chosen to reproduce this title even though it may possibly have occasional imperfections such as missing and blurred pages, missing text, poor pictures, markings, dark backgrounds and other reproduction issues beyond our control. Because this work is culturally important, we have made it available as a part of our commitment to protecting, preserving and promoting the world's literature. Thank you for your understanding.

THE
LITTLE CORPORAL.

A COMIC OPERA

IN THREE ACTS.

LIBRETTO BY HARRY B. SMITH.

MUSIC BY LUDWIG ENGLANDER.

AS PRESENTED BY THE

FRANCIS WILSON OPERA CO.

NEW YORK AND LONDON:
BREITKOPF & HAERTEL.

COPYRIGHTED 1898, BY HARRY B. SMITH.

THE LITTLE CORPORAL.

CHARACTERS.

THE MARQUIS DE ST. ANDRÉ, a proscribed nobleman acting as a leader of the uprising of Breton peasants against the French Republic.
PIERRE PETITPAS, servant of the Marquis de St. André.
JACQUES GROGNARD, sergeant of grenadiers.
AMULET BEY, a Mameluke chieftain.
GILET, a regimental tailor.
JEAN NIGAUD, a village cobbler.
URBAN, the village blacksmith.
ROGER NICOLE, a tavern keeper.
CORPORAL VIGNON.
CORPORAL RENARD.
JEAN FALCON, a Chouan leader.
JACQUELINE, the belle of a Breton village.
ADELE DE TOURVILLE, foster sister of Jacqueline.
SULTANETTA,
NEPHTALI,
GOULCHADE,
KASSIME,
} wives of Amulet Bey.
AGENOR.
MUSARON,
} drummer boys.
BABETTE, a village girl.
GENERAL MURAT.
   "   KLEBER.
   "   LANNES.
   "   JUNOT.
EUGENE DE BEAUHARNAIS
ISHMAEL, an old Arab.

THE LITTLE CORPORAL.

ACT I.

A fishing village on the coast of Brittany. The right side of the stage is occupied by the Château de St. André, building of the sixteenth century architecture. The walls are partly covered by moss and vines. The Château has an appearance romantic and mysterious, as if it had been deserted for some time. At left is the cottage of the village blacksmith with a forge. Further down stage is the cottage of the village tailor. At the back of the stage are rocks and a strip of beach, beyond which the sea is seen.

Two Breton peasants, an old man and a boy, are caulking an old boat. Four peasants, two men and two boys, are hauling in a seine. On the highest point of the rocks at back, two peasant girls are looking out upon the sea, shading their eyes and talking together as if watching a ship in the distance. In front of the cabaret NIGAUD, GILET, URBAN *and* ROGER *are drinking.*

At left sits a man carving wooden shoes. Two peasant girls are mending nets.

No. I.—BRETON FISHERMAN'S SONG.

SOLO.	St. Simon was a fisher-man,
CHORUS.	(Sing ho yo! and a heave-a-ho!)
SOLO.	Into his net the fishes ran.
CHORUS.	(Sing ho yo! and a heave-a-ho!)
SOLO.	He only had to pray to get
	A ton of herring in his net.
SEMI-CHORUS.	Such luck as his we never met,
	(Sing cheerily, merrily heave-a-ho!)

(The distant chiming of the Angelus is heard. The peasants all stop their work; the men take off their caps; all bow their heads for a moment, while the bells are heard through orches-

tral symphony. *Then all resume work and take up the second stanza of the song. During this second stanza the bells are heard in the distance.*)

SOLO.	St. Simon was so good a man
SEMI-CHORUS.	(Sing ho yo! and a heave-a-ho!)
SOLO.	He never used a frying-pan,
SEMI-CHORUS.	(Sing ho yo! and a heave-a-ho!)
FULL CHORUS.	He said a pray'r upon the spot,
	Then hauled his net and found a lot
	Of fine fried fish all piping hot.
	(Sing marry good masters, such luck is rare.)

(URBAN *at table, rapping with tankard.*)

    Rap—rap—rap—rap! Babette come here!
    Our cups are low. Fill up my dear!
GILET. And when we drink, a toast's the thing!
    I'll give you one! My friends—the king!
ALL (*loudly*). The king!
AN OLD PEASANT. Hush! Not so loud!
ALL (*softly*). The king!

(*All having tankards drink. The cry of an owl is heard in the distance. All listen. The owl cry is heard nearer.*)

CHORUS (*sotto voce*).
    'Tis the cry of the Chouans! Some danger is near.
    Hush! Hush! Hush!
BABETTE (*up stage*). 'Tis a friend who's drawing near.
    There's nothing to fear.
ALL (*gladly*). Friends! Friends!

(JEAN FALCON, *a Chouan leader, appears over the rocks. He is wounded, and has a bandage around his head. He carries a musket.*)

JEAN FALCON. None of the Blues about? No spies?
CHORUS. None! None!

(*A party of Chouans enter. They are all rough peasants, bronzed, their hair unkempt. Their garments are partly of coarse linen, partly of goat-skin. Some wear cowhide boots, some wooden shoes. Some wear a Breton hat; some wear caps; some have handkerchiefs tied around their heads. They are greeted by the peasants.*)

JEAN FALCON. Speak, is the coast quite clear?
CHOUANS. Ay, ay!
JEAN FALCON. Someone, my friends, is here?
ALL. Someone? Then say who can this someone be?
JEAN. Hist! 'Tis a guest I dare not name;
    The lord of the château!
CHORUS. The Marquis?

JEAN. The same!
CHORUS (*with enthusiasm*). The Marquis hail!

(THE MARQUIS DE ST. ANDRÉ *rushes in. He is dressed as a Chouan leader. All surround him.*)

MARQUIS. Friends! Comrades! Once again we meet.
With joy your faithful hearts I greet.
Loyal souls, let us advance,
And give once more a King to France!

ROYALIST WAR SONG.—ST. ANDRE AND CHORUS.

I.

Do you hear the voice that's calling you in ev'ry breeze that blows?
It is throbbing like a bugle through the air,
'Tis whispering of treachery; 'tis muttering of foes
Who have brought our land to terror and despair.
The voice is like a rolling drum heard faintly from afar,
A distant trumpet sounding the advance;
And at even in the southward there's a red and flaming star,
'Tis a signal to the loyal sons of France.

Sons of France, awake, arise!
For sabres your plowshares bring.
Loyalty your watchword! Victory your prize!
Fight for the right and the King!
Sons of France, your hour is nigh.
To the faith of your fathers cling.
Rise in your might! Conquer or die
For the King, sons of France! For the King!

II.

They have robbed us of the lilies on the banner white and gold,
They have given us a standard red as flame,
And the sons that gave our nation all its glories manifold,
They have given unto death and unto shame.
The worship of our fathers they have banished from the land,
And Death awaits to serve the tyrant's voice.
For the sceptre they have given us the bayonet and the brand,
Let us fight them with the weapons of their choice.

Sons of France, awake! Arise!
 For sabres your plowshares bring,
Loyalty your watchword! Victory your prize!
 Fight for the right and the King!
Sons of France, your hour is nigh,
 To the faith of your fathers cling.
Rise in your might! Conquer or die
 For the King, sons of France! For the King!

*   *   *   *   *   *   *   *

No. II.—JEANETTE, THE FARMER'S DAUGHTER.

SONG.—Jacqueline.

I

Jeanette, the farmer's daughter
 Was ever merry and fair
(*Sing marry-come up, my dearies,*
 For the farmer's daughter fair).
Two rival suitors sought her,
 Gros Jean and P'tit Pierre
(*Sing marry come-up, my dearies,*
 For Gros Jean and P'tit Pierre).
Gros Jean was old and stupid and cold,
But Jean had lots of silver and gold,
While a laughing eye that was bad and bold,
 Had gallant and gay P'tit Pierre.
   Ohé!
For merry and bold P'tit Pierre.

 O la, la, la! O la, la, la!
  You sad coquette, Jeanette!
 O la, la, la! O la, la, la!
  She made those lovers fret.
 Ha, ha! ho, ho, for poor Pierre!
  She left him in the lurch,
 And with Jean, the rich old simpleton,
  She trotted off to church.

II.

Jeanette went flaunting gaily,
 In velvet and satin so rare
(*Sing marry-come-up, my dearies,*
 For her rustling silks so rare!).
Gros Jean to market daily
 Drove his old doddering mare.
(*Sing lack-a-day! How lame alway*
 Was that most ancient mare!)

So long the way 'twould take all day
To drive to town with that mare so gray;
Jeanette alone was afraid to stay,
   So she sent for gay P'tit Pierre
     To share
The lot of a fair solitaire.

   O la, la, la ! O la, la, la !
     You sad coquette, Jeanette !
   O la, la, la ! O la, la, la !
     Gros Jean is guessing yet.
   Ha, ha ! ho, ho ! When that gray nag
     Is far across the hills,
   Pierre, he pays her visits, while
     Gros Jean, he pays her bills.

*   *   *   *   *   *   *   *

No. III. DUET.—ADELE AND ST. ANDRÉ.

ST. ANDRÉ.	An exile is my heart,
	  Compelled to roam
	In lonely lands and strange
	  Afar from home,
	And as my eyes turn homeward still,
	  Wherever I may rove,
	This banished heart of mine returns
	  Unto its true first love.

ADELE.	That love is true, whatever Fate
	  For thee is keeping
	  Of joy or weeping,
	Whatever chance and change await,
	  It shall not fail thee,
	  Though storms assail thee.
	When night is dark—a star to guide thee
	  Until the peril all is gone.
	A watch I'll keep lest harm betide thee
	  Until the coming of the dawn.

BOTH.	One love is true, whatever Fate
	  For thee is keeping
	  Of joy or weeping,

ST. ANDRÉ.	Through all the storms of life to guide me An angel pure to watch beside me.
BOTH.	O dear first love, if I but know That thou art true for aye to me,

My courage, then, shall never fail me.
    But in the fight
      For truth and right
    I'll ever faithful be.

*   *   *   *   *   *   *   *

No. IV.—THE COBBLER'S GHOST.

SONG.—PETITPAS.

I.

As Jean Nigaud, the cobbler, sat
  Before his shop one day,
And at a pair of hobnailed boots
  He gaily tapped away,
The blue-coats marching down the street,
  Espied the luckless knave,
And then and there insisted that
  He seek a soldier's grave.

He cried, "I'm very busy
  With my rap-tap, tap-tap-tap.
And marching makes me dizzy,
  I would rather rap-tap-tap."
In vain did poor Jean fume and fret,
A scant ten minutes he could get
To say good-bye to his Babette,
  With a rap-tap, rap-tap-tap.

Adieu, Babette ma belle,
  And if perchance I'm slew,
Don't wed another fellow, or
  My ghost will worry you.
My spectre'll sit beside your bed,
  And mar your nuptial nap,
By making ghostly boots and shoes
  With a ghastly rap-rap-rap.

II.

He fought a lot did Jean Nigaud;
  He lost an arm, a leg;
He substituted for the same
  A hook and wooden peg.
He lost an eye; he lost an ear;
  Of teeth he'd half a set.
At last he wandered homeward and
  He hunted up Babette.

To his old shop a-hobbling;
　Then he heard a rap-tap-tap.
Another chap sat cobbling,
　With his rap tap, tap-tap-tap.
That cobbler said: "I'm glad we've met
A hero; and my wife shall get
A drink for you. Come here, Babette!"
　What a rap-tap, rap-tap-tap!

"So so, Babette, coquette!
　You could not wait for me."
"I would not be the better half
　Of half a man," said she.
"You have one foot in the grave,"
　She said, "My poor old chap.
I couldn't stand that wooden leg
　With its rap-tap-tap-tap-tap."

III.

Of course he went and hanged himself,
　His dread revenge to wreak.
That night when fair Babette awoke,
　She gave a gruesome shriek;
A shriek that woke her honored spouse,
　And in the moonlight dim
They saw the ghost of Jean Nigaud—
　Or what was left of him.

A pair of brogans making,
　With a rap-tap-tap-tap-tap,
He set them quaking, shaking,
　With his rap-tap-tap-tap-tap.
He grinned and gibbered with delight.
Imagine if you can their fright.
He came thereafter every night,
　With his rap-tap, rap-tap-tap!

"So so, Babette, coquette,
　You couldn't wait, my dear;
How do you like a one-eyed ghost
　Who's lost his larboard ear?
At twelve o'clock each night
　I'll come and spoil your nap,
A dismal spook with peg and hook,
　And a rap-tap-tap-tap-tap."

*　*　*　*　*　*　*　*

No. V.—RUSTIC DUET.

Petitpas and Jacqueline.

I.

JACQUELINE. Within a cote our door above,
We'll keep full many a snowy dove,
Whose plaintive, pensive "coo-coo-coo"
Will tell us tales of love.

PETITPAS. We will not think it *infra dig*,
To also keep a little pig;
Methinks I hear its "Ugh-ugh-ugh,"
A clean one, not too big.

JACQUELINE. Of turkeys we must have a few,
They are such tender friends and true;
Their merry, gladsome "glou-glou-glou"
Is lovely music, too.

PETITPAS. We'll keep a dog which tramps will mark,
Whose hoarse but highly honest bark
Will, by its savage "wow-wow-wow,"
Scare prowlers after dark.

(*Refrain.*)

We shall go to sleep at dark,
We shall waken when the lark
With his very early carol gives us warning,
And the music we shall love,
Every melody above,
Shall be the plowboy's whistle in the morning.

II.

JACQUELINE. Upon our little farm we'll keep
A little flock of little sheep,
To sing to us their "baa-baa-baa,"
And soothe to balmy sleep.

PETITPAS. We'll keep amid those scenes of peace
A little flock of little geese,
To warble to us "quack-quack-quack"
Until we bid them cease.

JACQUELINE. Upon our little field will browse
A little coterie of cows
To cheer us with their "moo-moo-moo"
As gaily they carouse.

PETITPAS. While little hens, both white and grey,
Wil soothe us with their little lay;
We'll hear their lively "cluck-cluck-cluck"
Through all the livelong day.

(*Refrain.*)

We shall go to sleep at dark,
We shall waken when the lark
With its very early carol gives us warning,
And the music that we love,
Every melody above,
Shall be the plowboy's whistle in the morning.
(*Sabot dance.*)

* * * * * * * *

(GROGNARD, *his coat and one boot off, sits on a three-legged stool.* GILET, *the tailor, sits cross-legged on the ground and mends* GROGNARD'S *coat.* NIGAUD, *the cobbler, mends* GROGNARD'S *boot.* URBAN, *the blacksmith, at his forge, works at sharpening* GROGNARD'S *sword.*

No. IV. A GRENADIER'S SONG.—GROGNARD.

I.

Ho, Master Tailor, perch on your marrow bones,
  Patch up the coat where the bullet tickled me;
Sew up the seams so the coat will last a year or two;
  Charge it to France, and a patriot you'll be.
See, Master Cobbler, boots could not be sorrier;
  Bad at the heels, aye, and worse at the toes.
Make 'em so strong they can carry a warrior
  Half 'round the world if the tri-color goes.

Oh, a tailor's meek,
And a cobbler's weak,
Like a couple of grandams old.
It's right they should work
In their meek, weak way
For the men who are brave and bold.
Peg away and sew,
For the work, you know,
Is for one of your bold defenders.
Coat and boots shall share
In the fame of the guard
That dies but never surrenders.

II.

Ho, Master Blacksmith, blow me a mighty blast,
  Blow me a blast till the forge is in a flame.
Mend me the sword that was broken on the enemy;
  Charge it to France—you will get your pay in fame.

Strike me a blow there, and strike me a lusty one:
　Swing that big arm of yours. Do the best you know.
The sabre you hold there has e'er been a trusty one;
　The edge that you sharpen was blunted on the foe.

　　　Let the strong arm swing,
　　　　And the hammer ring,
　　Till the sabre's done for me;
　　　　Each blow that you strike
　　　　Is a blow for France,
　　And shall help us make you free.
　　　　For that steel, I swear,
　　　　Aye shall win its share
　　Of our new Republic's splendors.
　　　　It shall share in the fame
　　　　Of the brave Old Guard
　　That dies but never surrenders.

(*The tavern keeper*, ROGER NICOLE, *enters, carrying a jug of liquor to the château.* GROGNARD *stops him.* BABETTE *enters.*)

　Ho, Master Boniface, fill me a cup or two.
　　Mind you, the best wine is none too good, my man.
Don't speak of cash! You are honored when I drink with you.
　　Charge it to France; she will pay you when she can.
You little girl with the starry eyes and ebon hair,
　Lend me your waist for a roving arm or two.
Pay France's soldiers with smiles sweet and debonair.
　Give me a kiss; 'tis the least that you can do.

　　　　For it's only fair,
　　　　So it is, I swear,
　　That the men who fight for France
　　　　Should drink of her best,
　　　　And make love to her girls,
　　For it's rarely they have the chance.
　　　　So give a kiss
　　　　To a soldier, miss;
　　To one of yon bold defenders.
　　　　It's all for the sake
　　　　Of the brave Old Guard
　　That dies but never surrenders.

*　　*　　*　　*　　*　　*　　*　　*

NO. VII.—DRILL SONG.

PETITPAS, GROGNARD AND CHORUS.

CHORUS.　　Hay-foot! Straw-foot! Left, left!
PETITPAS.　Left a wife and seven children,
　　　　　　Left my loving aunts and cousins
　　　　　　　　On my 'listing day.

CHORUS.	Hay-foot! Straw-foot! Left, left!
PETITPAS.	Left my weeping friends by dozens,
	Left a happy home behind me
	When I marched away.

I.

GROGNARD.	Bugles are a-braying,
	Champing steeds are neighing.
	Here's your musket ready; you must take it.
PETITPAS.	I would surely plague you
	For I've got the ague.
	If I joined the army I would shake it.
GROGNARD.	Ev'ry heart is thrilling
	With the zeal for killing.
	Warriors of France there is no matching.
PETITPAS.	I don't feel the thrillness;
	But I've several kinds of illness,
	And ev'ry blessed one of 'em is catching.

(Refrain.)

GROGNARD.	March away to battle! On to do or die.
PETITPAS.	Crikey! How I hate to leave my mother.
GROGNARD.	Charge upon the foeman! Tyranny defy.
PETITPAS.	Wishes I could send my little brother.
GROGNARD.	Victory or death, boys! Glory or the grave!
PETITPAS.	Hang the luck! home cooking I shall miss,
	And I wish that I may die if another scrape I try
	If so be as I should once get out of this.

II.

GROGNARD.	Let us go and perish,
	Fame our names shall cherish.
	Epitaphs and monuments delight us.
PETITPAS.	I am very sick. It's
	Housemaid's knee and rickets;
	Also I've a soupçon of St. Vitus.
GROGNARD.	When you die in glory
	We shall tell your story,
	Weeping with emotion paroxysmal.
PETITPAS.	Please to let me off, sir,
	I've a nasty cough, sir.
	Listen, sir, to this, now! Ain't it dismal?

(Refrain.)

GROGNARD.	March away to battle! On to do or die!
PETITPAS.	Crikey! How I 'ates to leave my mother—
	Etc.

* * * * * * * *

NO. VIII.—FINALE.

Four Girls (*hauling nets*).

St. Simon was a fisherman,
Into his net the fishes ran—

(Grognard *suddenly interrupts angrily.*)

Grognard. Stop that racket! Devil take ye!
Stop it, peasants, or I'll make ye!

Peasant. What's this? A fleet at anchor yonder!
And one ship drawing near!
What does it mean, I wonder?
Grognard. The fleet! The fleet is here.

Sound the roll on the drum!
Bid the men hither come!
We must embark
Ere it is dark.

(*Drum rolls. Laughter of the soldiers is heard off in the castle.*)

Men (*boisterously*). Ho, ho, ho, ho, ho!
Grognard (*angrily*). Those rascally plunderers!
Men (*laughing*). Ho, ho, ho, ho, ho!
Grognard. Such bandits and blunderers!
If the General finds this out,
I shall lose my stripes, no doubt!

Grognard.	Men (*laughing*).
Plunderers! Blunderers!	Ho, ho, ho! Ho, ho, ho!

(*The men enter from the castle, all laughing uproariously. They are laden with the spoils of the castle. Two are dressed in parts of a suit of old rusty armor and carry battle-axes. Two have on old velvet robes trimmed with ermine. One has on an old helmet, and a woman's robe flung over his shoulder. One carries a shield and spear. One has an antique crossbow. Several have sacks flung over their shoulders containing vases and other bric à-brac. One wears a full court wig. Two carry large portraits of the ancestors of* St. André. *As they march on all sing mockingly.*)

Chorus of Men.
March away to battle! On to do or die.
Crikey, how we hate to leave our mothers,
Charge upon the foeman! Tyranny defy.
Wishes we could send our little brothers.
Victory or death, boys! Glory or the grave!
Hang the luck! home cooking we shall miss,

And we wishes we may die if another scrape we try
If so be as we should once get out of this.
  Ha, ha! Ho, ho!
(*Shouting*) Vive la Republique!

(*They place helmets, hats and wigs on guns or spears and wave them frantically.* GROGNARD *is furious. Melodrame as a soldier drags the* MARQUIS *from the castle and whirls him to centre. A corporal follows, dragging* PETITPAS, *who is thrown to centre.* PETITPAS *is grotesquely dressed and made up as a learned professor. Wearing a huge pair of green spectacles and a Dr. Syntax wig, he carries an armful of old books. The* MARQUIS *is also dressed as a scientific professor with eccentric make-up, wig and wide felt hat. As* PETITPAS *is whirled to centre the books scatter. There is a pause in the music here.*)

(*Dialogue.*)

(*Music resumed.*)

SAILORS (*off stage*).	Ahoy! Ahoy!
PRINCIPALS (*on stage*).	The brig is near!
ALL.	Ahoy! Ahoy!
	Good landing here!

(*They signal off at back. Melodrame for the entrance of the ship at back.*)

ALL (*as the ship comes on*).	Ahoy! Ahoy!
	Huzza! Huzza!

(*Tableau.*)

GROGNARD (*recit*).	Now farewell to friends and home.
ALL.	A last farewell!

(*Ensemble.*)

Adieu, a fond adieu,
O, dearest land of France.
We leave our hearts with thee
In one last parting glance.
Adieu, a fond adieu,
We'll ne'er return, perchance;
But we shall win thee glory,
O, lovely land of France.

JACQUELINE.	Now up with the anchor
	And up with the sail!
	Ho, yo, ho! There's a favoring gale.
ALL.	All aboard! All aboard!

(*Waltz ensemble.*)

 O'er the world we'll bear thee,
  Tri-color of France.
 Win for thee full many a fight
  Thy glory to enhance.
 That loved flag shall be unfurled
 In the distant Eastern world.
  Shining afar
  E'en as the star
 That leads our General on.
  Fighting for liberty,
  Fighting for victory,
   True sons of France,
   Onward! Advance!

PETITPAS (*aside*).

 This warrior business is not in my line,
 I feel creepy chills promenading my spine.

JACQUELINE (*aside to Petitpas*).

 Come, courage! Take heart, lad, and do not be glum,
 I'll tone up your nerves with a roll on my drum.
   Rat a plan-plan-plan.

CHORUS.   Rat-a-plan-plan-plan.

 O'er the world we'll bear thee,
  Tri-color of France, etc.

 Then up with the flag!
 And up with the sail!
  Ho for the sea
 With a fav'ring gale.

  Vive la Republique!
   Huzza!
   Huzza!

(*Tableau. The peasant soldiers kiss their wives and mothers good-bye. The regular soldiers kiss the young girls. The* MARQUIS *in pantomime begs* ADELE *to stay, but she goes to the ship and signals for him to follow.* PETITPAS *attempts to sneak off, but* GROGNARD *seizes him and orders him to the ship; he catches the eye of* JACQUELINE, *who shames him for his cowardice. He then takes courage and marches boldly to the ship.* PETITPAS *hoists the tri-color flag as the ship sails. Tableau.*)

END OF ACT I.

ACT II.

A market place in the city of Alexandria; streets in perspective. At right a house used as Bonaparte's headquarters. The tri-color flag hangs draped from a balcony. At left are buildings used as regimental barracks; also with the French tri-color. Further up stage at left is the booth of a fruit seller, and opposite this, at right, is the booth of a merchant of bric à brac.

At the moment the scene is disclosed there is a burst of cheering from all on the stage, " Vive Bonaparte! Vive le General!" In the foreground is an old Arab woman seated on a rug telling fortunes to two Bedouins. Opposite is a snake-charmer giving an exhibition. With the exception of these two groups the female chorus is massed at the back of the stage watching the passing of the French army, which crosses the stage at the back; old battle flags flying; the sun shining on the bayonets. The watching crowd is made up of Arab women and youths of various types, dancing girls, musicians, pedlars, jugglers, merchants and beggars. Little is seen of the passing soldiers but their heads, as the crowd of natives obstructs the view. In the windows of the buildings are Arab women watching the passing troops. The passing soldiers toss their hats in air, twirl them on bayonets, throw kisses to Arab girls in the windows, marching with no discipline.

No. IX.—MALE CHORUS.

With a tramp-tramp-tramp
  And a plan-plan-plan,
Come warriors victorious
  Since first the war began.
With a tramp-tramp-tramp
  Our progress naught can bar,
We're led to battle glorious
  By our commander's star.
Lead us on—on—on
  While the brazen bugle sings,
Where the eagles of La France
  Bring glory on their wings,
Let us march—march—march
  To the honor that we prize.
As a soldier lives for glory
  'Tis for glory that he dies.

(*There is a loud fanfare of trumpets and roll of drums. The passing soldiers now join in the Marseillaise Hymn, which they sing with great enthusiasm. While the men are singing the Marseillaise, the women sing in counterpoint a melody Oriental in color and entirely contrasting with the martial spirit of the male chorus.*)

MEN.	WOMEN.
Allons, enfants de la Patrie!	Allah il Allah!
Le jour de gloire est arrivé;	Hear us, O mighty power!
Contre nous de la tyrannie	Allah defend us.
L'entendard sanglant est levé.	Now in our darkest hour.
Entendez vous, dans les campagnes	Tyranny's hand
Mugir les féroces soldats ?	Strangles us all.
Ils viennent, jusque dans nos bras,	See our fair land
Egorger nos fils, nos compagnes!	Fast in the thrall.
	Allah defend us!
Aux armes; mes citoyens!	Heed thou our call!
Formez vos battaillons	Drive the invader
Marchons, marchons, Qu'un sang impur,	Forth from thy shrine.
Abreuve nos sillons.	Guard us! Protect us,
	Ruler divine!

(*At the moment they sing "Aux armes, mes citoyens," GENERAL BONAPARTE passes at the back, riding a white horse. He is surrounded by a group of officers also on horseback. As he appears all the soldiers shout "Vive BONAPARTE!" An Arab appears in a window and takes deliberate aim at BONAPARTE. A Grenadier seeing this shoots the Arab, who falls back into the house. The Arab women cover their faces, and some threaten BONAPARTE with gestures. Two or three French soldiers threaten these women, who then pretend to join in the enthusiastic shouts.*)

*   *   *   *   *   *   *   *

No. X.—THE OLD WAR HORSE.

SONG.—JACQUELINE, GROGNARD AND CHORUS.

I.

GROGNARD.   A bold dragoon had an old grey nag,
                 An old war horse was he
              Who loved the rattle and roar of battle
                 As a drunkard loves a spree.

JACQUELINE.   He'd jog all day in a slouching way,
                 Quite feeble and meek and mild,
              But if ever he heard the trumpet sound
                 That old nag would just go wild.

GROGNARD.	GIRLS' CHORUS.
Yes, when he heard a trumpet,	Tan-ta-ra-ra-ra!
He'd just get up and hump it,	Tan-ta-ra-ra-ra!
He'd clatter like mad, a galloping, galloping	Ta-ra!
On where the fight was thick.	Ta-ra!
The rest might like or lump it,	Ta-ra!
If that horse heard a trumpet,	
He'd snort and prance and rear and dance,	MALE CHORUS.
Like an equine lunatic.	Galloping—galloping
	Galloping—galloping
	Etc.

ALL.   Ha ha! Ho ho!
Like an equine lunatic.

(*Refrain.*)

Of course it only goes to show
What all are supposed to know
That men are always habit's slaves,
When habits once they fix.
Just as the twig is bent we find.
The tree is sure to be inclined.
The shoemaker ever should stick to his last,
And you can't teach old dogs new tricks.

II.

GROGNARD.   There came a day when that war-horse grey
Was sold to a boorish clown
Of rustic ilk who peddled milk
And cream in a market town.

JACQUELINE.   That brave old nag was compelled to drag
A milk cart from early dawn;
With a step of lead and a drooping head,
All his warlike spirit gone.

GROGNARD.	GIRLS CHORUS.
But down the road one morning,	Tan-ta-ra-ra-ra!
The trumpets loud gave warning,	Tan-ta-ra-ra-ra!
A cavalry troop came galloping, galloping,	Ta-ra!
Galloping fine as silk.	Etc.
That nag began cavorting,	
Then bolted wildly snorting.	MALE CHORUS.
His old heels flew! The cans went too!	Rattlety—bang—bang!
And up went the price of milk.	Rattlety—bang—bang!

ALL.   Ha ha! Ho ho!
And up went the price of milk.

(*Refrain.*)

That old war horse he seemed to say,
In sad and reproachful way.
"Gunpowder and cream are things I deem
That never were made to mix."
Just as the twig is bent you'll find
The tree is sure to be inclined.
The shoemaker ever should stick to his last,
And you can't teach old dogs new tricks.

*   *   *   *   *   *   *   *

No. XI.—WE HAVEN'T DISCOVERED IT YET

TOPICAL SONG.—Petitpas and Chorus.

I.

PETITPAS. Although I'm a scientist fully as wise
   As any you'll find in the diocese,
  My head still continues its natural size,
   I've no cranial elephantiasis.
  I do not pretend to know ev'ry old thing.
   Au contraire, I admit, with regret,
  We cannot be sure about some things obscure,
   For we haven't discovered them yet.

(Refrain.)

CHORUS. What! You haven't discovered them yet? Oho!
PETITPAS. We tried to discover them years ago.
    We sought high and low,
    We sought to and fro;
   But still we have nothing to show,
  And so we're compelled to admit, with regret,
  There are things that we haven't discovered as yet.

(Encore verses ad libitum.)

* * * * * * * *

No. XII.—THE SONG OF THE LAMPOON.

Petitpas, St. André and Ensemble.

I.

ST. ANDRÉ. Upon a little island there
    Was born a little man;
   While he was in the cradle still
    To conquer he began.
PETITPAS. He smote his nurse and, what was worse,
    When he to christ'ning came
   He pulled the holy father's nose
    And laughed at parents' shame.
ST. ANDRÉ. When he was but a half-year old,
    If true the story told,
   He sighed and sobbed to get a chance
    To go and conquer France.
PETITPAS.   But he concluded, "No!
   I'll wait a year or so.
    I'll try a deeper game
    To win my name and fame."

CHORUS. Mironton! Mironton! Mirontaine!

(Refrain.)

Sing Ohé for this great little man;
He's making the whole world Corsican.
  He's bound to own
  A crown and throne—
Ay, that is his merry republican plan.

II.

St. André. He had of brothers half a score;
  Of sisters he'd a few.
He swore that ev'ry Bonaparte
  Should have a throne or two.
Petitpas. Then in a garret room he starved,
  Till wily Barras came,
And blandly said, "I wish you'd wed
  A lady I shall name."
St. André. Said Boney, "I shall wed, of course.
  My price a sword, a horse;
And General I should like to be
  To lead to Italy.
Petitpas. Thus with his lovely wife
  He got his start in life.
While wily Barras, you'll believe,
  Laughed softly in his sleeve.

Chorus. Mironton! Mironton! Mirontaine!

(Refrain.)

Sing Ohé for this great little man;
He's making the whole world Corsican.
  He's bound to own
  A crown and throne—
Ay, that is his wily republican plan.

*   *   *   *   *   *   *   *

No. XIII. DUET.—St. André and Adele.

I.

St. André.
Let me hold once more your hand in mine, dear;
 Once more let me look into your eyes.
Eyes within whose azure deeps divine, dear,
 Now the tears of tender love arise.
Parted by the night of trial and sorrow,
 We have waited long the dawn to see;
But for our sad love there is no morrow;
 All our hopes and dreams can never be.

BOTH.   Goodbye, sweetheart of mine,
            The dream is past;
        My love in memory's shrine
            Keep till the last.
        Life lies all fair before thee;
        In death, I bless, adore thee;
        My spirit shall watch o'er thee
            Where'er thou art.
            Goodbye, sweetheart.

ADELE.
        'Tis for right and loyalty you perish,
            Yielding up your life for faith and truth.
        While I live this heart of mine shall cherish
            Thee, the one dear love of days of youth.
        Death and fate may not our souls dissever.
            Like a star, thy love for me shall shine
        Faithful to the dear dead past forever,
            In the long, dark years that may be mine.

BOTH.   Goodbye, sweetheart of mine,
            The dream is past;
        My love in memory's shrine
            Keep till the last.
        Life lies all fair before thee;
        In death, I bless, adore thee;
        My spirit shall watch o'er thee
            Where'er thou art.
            Goodbye, sweetheart.

* * * * * * * *

No. XIV. THE SONG OF THE DRUM.—JACQUELINE AND CHORUS.

I.

Oh, here's a song for the drum;
For its voice has ne'er been dumb,
In France's glorious battles it has helped to win the day.
When the Bastille tumbled down,
When the Capet lost his crown,
The drum was there; to mark the time it gaily tapped away.

Then follow the drum, the rolling drum,
And you will conquerors become,
    With readiest rattle,
    Into the battle,
Leading where liberty's banners wave.

Ay, follow the drum, the rolling drum,
  When its music bids you come.
Mid flashing of steel and artillery's roar,
  Its voice is a song of war.

II.

A toast in praise of the drum.
It may bring dismay to some,
When after it the Grenadiers with flashing steel advance.
To Italy it led,
Where foemen fought and fled,
And Austria was humbled there before the flag of France.

  Then follow the drum, the rolling drum,
    And you will conquerors become.
      With readiest rattle,
      Into the battle,
  Leading where Liberty's banners wave.
  Ay, follow the drum, the rolling drum,
    When its music bids you come.
  Mid flashing of steel and artillery's roar,
    Its voice is the song of war.

*   *   *   *   *   *   *   *

No. XV.—FINALE.

AMULET BEY.
  Peering left and peering right,
    Come we Arabs stealthy.
  For the foe who comes in sight,
    'Twill be most unhealthy.
  For we're the Mamelukes bold, ha, ha!

ARABS.   Ha, ha! The Mamelukes fierce!
AMULET. Of valor uncontrolled, ha, ha!
ARABS.   With sword and lance to pierce.
AMULET. Hallali! We charge the foe,
  Like the rush of the hot simoon.
  Hallali! We lay them low;
  In the dust they lie full soon.

AMULET (*dancing*).
  Mamelukes, Mamelukes, Mamelukes we!
    Allah our battle cry!
      Our Kismet may
      Be death to-day;
  But the Franks shall also die.

ARABS (*dancing*).
  Hallali! Hallali! Hallali!
  Aye, the Frankish dogs shall die.
Mamelukes, Mamelukes, Mamelukes we!
    Etc.

(*They end the wild Bedouin dance with a pose, each threatening with his sword.*)
AMULET (*recit*).
    Into the house. Our prizes are there!
    The Frankish chiefs and their women fair.

(*Two Arabs drag on* ADELE *and* JACQUELINE. JACQUELINE *strikes the Arab who holds her. He threatens her with his scimitar. She faces him defiantly.*)

AMULET (*interfering*). No, no!
    The men who are rich and the girls who are handsome,
    Must not be injured, but kept for a ransom.

(*Melodrame as* ST. ANDRÉ *is dragged on struggling with two Arabs.*

ST. ANDRÉ. You Arab dogs! Release those ladies!
AMULET (*confronting* ST. ANDRÉ *satirically*).
    Be not alarmed fair sir,
     We gladly spare 'em;
    These damsels we intend
     Shall grace the harem.

JACQUELINE (*speaking*). The harem? *I?*
AMULET (*recit.*). But where the mighty Frankish chief?
    Great Bonaparte?
ALL (*as if trembling at the name*).
    Bonaparte! Bonaparte!

(*Melodrame.* PETITPAS, *still dressed as Bonaparte, appears on the balcony of the house at right. Behind him is a big, fierce-looking Bedouin with drawn scimitar.* PETITPAS, *terrified, swings from the balcony and drops. Two Arabs seize him and drag him to centre, where he trembles, desperately frightened.*)

AMULET (*savagely to* PETITPAS).
    We have thee, tyrant! Iron heart!
ALL ARABS. Slave of the devil! Bonaparte!

(PETITPAS *makes an effort to escape but is overpowered.*)

ARABS (*dancing*). Mamelukes, Mamelukes, Mamelukes we!
    Ha, ha! Etc.
AMULET. Now let's away before the Franks appear!
ARABS. Let's away—away—away!

(*Melodrame.* AMULET *and the Arabs about to lead the prisoners off.* JACQUELINE *gives a roll on the drum.* ST. ANDRÉ *blows a fanfare on a bugle, which he takes from its place on the wall. There is an answering roll of drums. Then a flourish of trumpets. Then shouts of "Vive la Republique." Two Arabs throw a cloak over the head of* PETITPAS *and drag him to left. He struggles grotesquely under the blanket. The French soldiers enter singing. As the French soldiers enter, led by* GROGNARD, *they group at right. The Arabs retreating to left, armed and threatening, determined to protect their prisoners, and especially guarding* PETITPAS. *Tableau.*)

FRENCH SOLDIERS, ST. ANDRÉ, GROGNARD, JACQUELINE, ADELE *and* PETITPAS.
  Lead us on —on—on.
    While the brazen bugle sings;
  Where the eagles of La France
    Bring glory on their wings.
  Let us march—march - march,
    To the honor that we prize;
  As a soldier lives for glory,
    'Tis for glory that he dies.

AMULET *and* ARABS.
  Allah il Allah!
  Accursed infidels!
  Thrice accursed Giaours!
  The foe of our nation!
    Etc., etc.

ST. ANDRÉ. Sons of France, awake and arise!
    Quick! To the rescue, we pray.
ST. ANDRÉ, JACQUELINE *and* ADELE.
    Our General's life in deadly peril lies.
    On to the charge! Don't delay.

FRENCH.
On to the charge!
  Allons! Allons!
Allons, enfants de la Patrie
  Le jour de gloire est arrivé;
Contre nous de la tyrannie
  L'etendard sanglant est levé.
Entendez-vous dans les campagnes
  Mugir ces feroces soldats?
Ils viennent jusque dans nos bras
  Egorger nos fils, nos compagnes.

Aux armes mes citoyens!
  Formez vos battaillons.
Marchons, marchons, Qu'un sang impur
  Abreuve nos sillons.

ARABS.
Repel the charge!
  The captives save!
Strike death to the invader
  With scimitar and sword.
We shall repel the infidel
  Who scorns the prophet's word.
No god is there but Allah,
  Mahomet is his prophet.
Strike, ye faithful! 'Tis the hour
  That dooms the Frankish Giaour!

Strike, ye faithful; strike
  With swords of fire and flame.
Put the Christian dogs to shame
  In great Mahomet's name.

AMULET. With the captives retreat—retreat!

(*The Arabs prepare to escape.*)

GROGNARD. Frenchmen! A rescue in the name of the Republic! Make ready!

(*The Grenadiers level their muskets at the Arabs, who thrust* JACQUELINE, ST. ANDRÉ *and* ADELE *before them to protect themselves.*)

GROGNARD. Aim!

(*As* GROGNARD *is about to order "Fire!"* PETITPAS *throws the cloak from his head, rushes in front of* ST. ANDRÉ, JACQUELINE *and* ADELE, *strikes a commanding attitude, and shouts:*)

PETITPAS. Soldiers! Don't fire! You will kill your General!

ENSEMBLE.

The French.	Arabs.

Victory! Victory!
  Shall yet be ours.
Vive la République!
	Victory! Victory!
	  O'er the Frankish Giaours.
	Allah il Allah!

(Tableau. The Arabs *are retreating under shelter of their prisoners. Two* Arabs *hold* St. André, *who struggles. An* Arab *holds* Jacqueline, *and one holds* Adele. *Two guard* Petitpas, *but do not touch him, leaving him free for a Napoleonic pose, confronting the French soldiers.* Amulet Bey, *beside* Petitpas, *thanks Allah that he has captured the great French commander, and points off to the desert. At right the French soldiers group, using the windows, doorway and balcony of the house. All leveling their muskets and ready to fire* Grognard, *commanding them, knocking up the guns of those nearest him, fearing* Bonaparte *will be hit. The* Arab *in charge of* Jacqueline *puts his arm around her. She draws a pistol and thrusts it in his face. He, frightened, falls.* Petitpas *puts his foot on the* Arab's *neck.* Amulet *threatens* Petitpas. *A soldier thrusts a tri-color flag into the hands of* Petitpas, *who holds it aloft with his left hand as he waves his sword with his right. As he strikes this pose a mirage appears, the picture occupying the entire back drop, and representing* Napoleon *crossing the desert with his soldiers.* Napoleon *is riding on a camel. On seeing this the French soldiers start in astonishment; some of the* Arabs *prostrate themselves in awe, and* Petitpas, *turning and seeing the picture with the real* Napoleon, *gives an exclamation of alarm, and falls into the arms of two* Arabs.)

END OF ACT II.

ACT III.

A Bedouin camp in an oasis in the desert. On the back drop is a view of the Pyramids and the great Sphinx. At right is a well, surrounded by grass, shrubs and palm trees. At left up stage is a statue of Memnon. Around the base of the statue are sand and rocks. At left is a camp fire. Back of the well at right is the tent of the chief, AMULET BEY. Two smaller tents up stage at left. It is early evening. On the drop the red sun is setting, sinking beyond the waste of sand.

Around the fire are grouped several ARABS cooking the evening meal. Around the well are groups of ARAB girls variously occupied, one or two of them drawing water from the well. Up stage two or three horses tethered. These may be led off during the opening chorus. Some of the girls are dancing and playing on Oriental instruments. The men, seated around the camp-fire, are smoking Oriental pipes. Two or three men are dressing the skins of animals which they have killed. The four wives of AMULET BEY, SULTANETTA, NEPHTALI, GOULCHADE and KASSIME, are also discovered playing on musical instruments.

No. XVI.—OPENING ENSEMBLE.

ALL. Here let us pitch our tents for the night,
    For the long day's march is done.
They may rest who have earned the right,
    When the battle is fought and won.
Here where the spring of the desert purls,
    'Neath the shade of the spreading palm,
The chibouk and the song of the Bedouin girls
    May the Mameluke heart becalm.

(*All turn toward the setting sun and chant the following.*)

    See! in the western sky our lord the sun
        Sinketh to rest.
    His golden chariot its course has run.
        Repose is blest.

Our lord the sun abandons us
    To starlight dim,
While we, his children, now attune
    His parting hymn.

(All prostrating themselves.)

Hail, O mighty power,
  May thy light never fail;
We thy children at the dawning hour
  Thy returning shall hail.
Hail, O mighty pow'r,
    All hail.

(The Hymn to the Sun is worked up to a climax. The music then changes to melodrame. AMULET BAY enters. He rides on at back, dismounts, tosses his spear to a servant, sends his horse off and turns to greet his wives, SULTANETTA, NEPHTALI, GOULCHADE and KASSIME, who enter and joyfully welcome him.)

A BEDOUIN SONG.—AMULET BEY AND CHORUS.

I.

AMULET.
    Where'er the Bedouin's tent arises
      In the desert sands,
    No matter where, his home is there;
      He hath not gold nor lands.
    He hath not gold nor lands.
    He only hath a wife or two,
      Who mingle love with fear,
    A gallant steed to serve his need,
      A scimitar and spear.

(Refrain.)

Oh, who is as free as an Arab chief,
  Lion of the plain and hawk of the air!
Mashalla! Where are the Frankish dogs?
  Let them follow us here if they dare.
Hi! Hallo! As I clatter away,
  I and my steed worth his weight in gold,
I'll mock with my laughter whoe'er follows after.
  Oh, who is as free as a Bedouin bold?

CHORUS.
    He'll mock with his laughter whoe'er follows after,
      Oh, who is as free as a Bedouin bold?

II.

AMULET.   Franks, ye may deny the prophet,
    Wage with us your wars;
    But you'll not defy our lances
    Nor our scimitars.
    Come, follow us, ye Christian dogs
    To this, our wild retreat;
    The vulture and the jackal wait
    Our welcome to complete.

(Refrain.)

ALL. Oh, who is as free as an Arab chief,
   Lion of the plain and hawk of the air?
   Mashalla! Where are the Frankish dogs?
   Let them follow us here if they dare.
   Hi! Hallo! As we clatter away,
   Each on a steed worth his weight in gold.
   We'll mock with our laughter whoe'er follows after.
   Oh, who is as free as a Bedouin bold?

* * * * * * * *

No. XVII.—QUINTETTE.

PETITPAS, SULTANETTA, NEPHTALI, GOULCHADE AND KASSIME.

I.

SULTANETTA. Oh, the love of a Bedouin maiden
    Is like the fierce simoon;
NEPHTALI. Like flaming torches
    It sears and scorches,
    It's victim withers soon.
PETITPAS. To waste such a heart love-laden
    On me were quite too bad.
    I've a manner uncouth,
    And I can't tell the truth;
    In fact, I'm a miserable cad.
GIRLS.   A cad?
    Too bad!
    A cad?
    How sad!
PETITPAS. I much regret to say I am a miserable cad.

(Refrain.)

PETITPAS. So shun me; so shun me!
FOUR GIRLS. How can I when you've won me?
PETIT. My temper is a thing of which the bravest are afraid.

FOUR GIRLS.   I'll let you drink, I'll let you smoke,
     And if your loving wife you choke
     I'll laugh ha, ha! and call it a joke
      Upon your Bedouin maid.

    (*Dance Interlude.*)

II.

SULTANETTA. Oh, the love of a Bedouin lady
     Is wild and unrestrained.
NEPHTALI. It's highly torrid,
     And vengeance horrid
    It wreaks when it's disdained.
PETITPAS. My past has been extremely shady,
    I think I need say no more.
     I've a record that's rough;
     I've a temper that's tough.
    What's more, I'm a nuisance and a bore.
FOUR GIRLS. We ne'er
     Have loved
     A bore
     Before.
PETITPAS. Oh, yes; I am considered an unmitigated bore.

    (*Refrain.*)

PETITPAS. Don't choose me. Refuse me.
FOUR GIRLS. No, no. You cannot lose me.
PETIT. My morals are a total wreck, my intellect low grade.
FOUR GIRLS. A lack of brains we do not bar.
    We do not know what morals are.
    You're welcome quite with all your faults unto
     your Bedouin maid.

* * * * * * * *

No. XVIII.—THE ABSENT-MINDED GIRL.

SONG.—JACQUELINE.

I.

I knew an absent-minded girl,
 An artless little pet.
She always went out walking when
 The streets were damp and wet.
Her foot was neat, her ankle trim,
 But she was not aware,
So—absent mindedly—she'd show,
 Well, just about—to *there*.

(*Refrain.*)

Oh, my! Oh, fie!
Could she explain? She dared not try.
Poor dear! 'Twas clear
That it looked extremely queer.
That she should be
So careless it was sad to see;
Yet no one ever dared upbraid
That absent minded maid.

II.

She had a charming little hand—
  A fact she did not know,
And when she had her rings all on
  She'd hold that hand out—*so*.
But if one chanced to take her hand
  In his, she'd start afraid,
And blushing, say: "Please go—away,"
  That absent-minded maid.

  Oh, my! Oh, fie! etc.

III.

In absent-minded maiden way
  With some rich youth she'd stroll
On moonlight nights in shady nooks;
  She never thought, poor soul.
And if his lips approached her own,
  She no attention paid;
She'd be thinking then of something else,
  That absent-minded maid.

  Oh, my! Oh, fie! etc.

* * * * * * * *

No. XX.—FINALE.

* * * * * * * *

END OF THE OPERA.

Printed by WILLIAM GREEN, 324 to 330 Pearl Street, New York.

Printed by Libri Plureos GmbH in Hamburg,
Germany